YUKON
REFLECTIONS

Studio North Ltd.
Yukon, Canada

PHOTOGRAPHY BY WAYNE TOWRISS

Photography by Wayne Towriss

Book design by Steve Penner
Printed and bound in Canada
by Friesens, Altona, Manitoba.

ISBN 1-55056-511-7 (bound)
ISBN 1-55056-762-4 (pbk)

INTRODUCTION

Twenty-five years ago, and more, a young couple from the prairies of Saskatchewan moved to the Yukon, wanting to see more of northern Canada and expecting to stay two or three years.

The people of the territory and the rough mountainous landscape took them in, made them feel welcome, and soon they were well past the three year mark, had added two children and a dog to the family and knew that Yukon was home.

It is not an unusual story. The Yukon has been working its magic on visitors since the mid 1800's. Ancestors of those who trekked over the Chilkoot Trail to the Klondike in 1898 still reside in the territory. In fact those who trace their ancestry to the people who crossed the Bering Sea land bridge many thousands of years ago, still call Yukon home.

It may seem strange, but this rough, beautiful area in Canada's northwest has large numbers of former Saskatchewan residents, as well as many from the country's east coast. For years these two areas have formed the nucleus of those seeking jobs and a new home in the territory. The population continues to grow and is now over 31,000, with 23,000 in the capital city, Whitehorse.

Each summer tourists, also numbering in the thousands, head up the Inside Passage by water, or pilot their land yachts up the Alaska Highway, heading for adventure in the Yukon and Alaska. As it has been since the gold rush, the words "Yukon", "Klondike", and "Alaska", create mental images of high mountains full of wildlife and clear rivers and crystal lakes full of fish. The Yukon is one of the few places left where "the real world" can match the pictures in the mind. Hopefully this book will provide a hint of the beauty that the Yukon has to offer those willing to look.

The frontal ranges of Kluane National Park are year-round playgrounds. They provide hiking, mountain climbing, skiing and numerous other recreational possibilities, all in a spectacular wilderness setting.

The world famous Watson Lake Signposts were started by a homesick U.S. Army G.I. working on the construction of the Alaska Highway. The 10,000th sign was erected in 1990 and each year the travelling public adds more signs.

The Alaska Highway, constructed as a wartime measure during a nine-month period in 1942, connects Dawson Creek, B.C., and Fairbanks, Alaska. At the time it was little more than a 1400 mile trail through the wilderness. Today it is an all-season highway through one of the most scenic areas of North America.

Marsh Lake, just south of Whitehorse, is a spring staging area for Trumpeter Swans, Tundra Swans and other waterfowl awaiting open water in the Arctic. The first birds usually arrive in March.

OVERLEAF – **A** beaver pond is lit with the autumn colours of the Richthofen Valley, just south of Fox Lake, along the Klondike Highway.

A small flock of Tundra Swans rests on a pond near Haines Junction during a late spring snow flurry.

On the North Canol Road smoke from a forest fire hundreds of miles away turns Dragon Lake fireweed pink. The 624-mile Canol road and pipeline were built during the Second World War to supply oil from Norman Wells, N.W.T., to a refinery in Whitehorse.

The Canol Road, although winding and covered in gravel, provides access to one of the most beautiful, rugged areas of the Yukon.

Lapie Lake, along the South Canol Road. The South Canol is that portion of the road from Johnson's Crossing to Ross River and the North Canol is from Ross River to Norman Wells, N.W.T.

The midnight
sun sets over a
small, unnamed
lake along the
Alaska Highway.

Fall colours reflect in a pond along the North Canol Road.

Frost forms delicate patterns on a winter window.

OVERLEAF – **D**eserted log cabins beside the Mendenhall
River are only a short walk from the Alaska Highway.

Winter's -40 degree temperatures coat trees in frost.

Dwarf Fireweed, also known as River Beauty, adds a blaze of colour to the Yukon landscape during July and August.

The early morning sun mirrors Sheep Mountain in the quiet waters of Kluane Lake. The mountain is home to a flock of Dall Sheep that sometimes numbers up to 200 animals.

The largest and longest valley glaciers in Canada are found in Kluane National Park. Their massive weight causes these glaciers to flow to the lower outer ranges.

Only eighteen miles from the Alaska Highway, the Kaskawulsh Glacier is Kluane's most accessible. Part of the melt water from the glacier forms the Slims River, which flows into Kluane Lake, and part drains south to the Alsek River.

Fireweed frames one of several deserted log buildings at Silver City. Located on the south end of Kluane Lake, Silver City was established by gold mining activity in the region just after the turn of the century. In 1904 a wagon road connected it to Whitehorse. This trail became part of the Alaska Highway.

Much of the Yukon has been burned over by forest fires. For years after a fire, charred logs form an attractive background for new growth.

Kluane Lake mirrors the snow-capped mountains of the national park. These warmer ranges on the edge of the icefields are home to what may be the largest variety of wildlife in northern Canada.

Known for its storms, Kluane Lake is seldom this calm. On this, the largest lake in the territory, winds have miles to churn up huge waves.

For thousands of years the grassy foothills along the shore of Kluane Lake have provided ample grazing to moose, Grizzly Bear, Black Bear, Dall Sheep, caribou, and many smaller animals.

A canoe sits ready for an outing. Although summers are short, water sports are a favourite pastime for Yukoners and visitors.

Hundreds of people enjoy rafting the famous Tatshenshini River on short day trips. Others float the river system all the way to the Pacific.

Grizzlies enjoy the Yukon flora.

So do smaller creatures.

Melting spring snow forms patterns in the mountains of the Kluane Range.

Mountains of Alsek Pass are home to Mountain Goats as well as Dall Sheep. The region also has a large concentration of Grizzly Bear.

Kluane National Park contains some of the highest peaks in North America.
In 1980 the park and the neighbouring Wrangell-St. Elias National Park in
Alaska were commemorated as a United Nations World Heritage Site.

In the sky for only a few hours each day, the winter sun adds sparkle to the grandeur of the Kluane Ranges. The Alaska Highway parallels these mountains between Haines Junction and Kluane Lake.

Dall rams find spring grazing along the Slims River. Loess, the powdered rock from the glaciers, is rich in minerals and is distributed over the area by the wind, improving the range.

A Dall ewe and her lamb on Sheep Mountain. The lambs are born in late May or early June. Kluane Park contains approximately five thousand sheep, a fifth of the entire Yukon population.

Autumn colours surround Dezadeash Lake.

A storm mutes the autumn colour near
Beloud Post on the Haines Road.

Winter comes early in Kluane country. Mt. Worthington is reflected as ice forms in Kathleen
Lake. The lake is better known for its wind-whipped whitecaps than its reflections.

On warmer days this spot on the Kathleen River is frequented by anglers.

OVERLEAF — **A** small unnamed lake.

A crisp fall morning on a quiet Kathleen Lake inlet.

An early snow squall storms across Kathleen Lake. Old
burns surrounding the lake provide ideal habitat for moose.

Ice covers Kluane Lake as early as mid-October until the first weeks of June. This photo shows the lake and Sheep Mountain in November, the month when majestic Dall rams return to the mountain to fight for breeding privileges.

A fisherman tries his luck in Kluane. The lake takes its name from an Indian word that means "place of many fish."

In spite of ear-searing temperatures, the Stewart River often remains open into November.

As temperatures dip to -40 degrees, hoar frost turns much of the Yukon into a winter wonderland.

The beauty of Yukon autumn may be short-lived. Wind can turn a golden lake shore leafless brown overnight.

Five Finger Rapids was a Yukon River hazard to rough-hewn Klondike Gold Rush craft and to sternwheeler traffic in later years. On their upstream struggle, the steamers navigated the smallest channel with the aid of winches and cables.

In this aerial photo, Carcross can be seen at the narrows between Bennet Lake on the right and Nares Lake on the left. The Klondike Highway (also known as the Carcross-Skagway Road) winds along the lake shore on its way to tidewater in Alaska.

Emerald Lake is situated along the Klondike Highway between Carcross and Whitehorse; few go by without stopping to admire the view. The lake's rainbow colours are caused by light waves reflecting from the white sediment on its bottom.

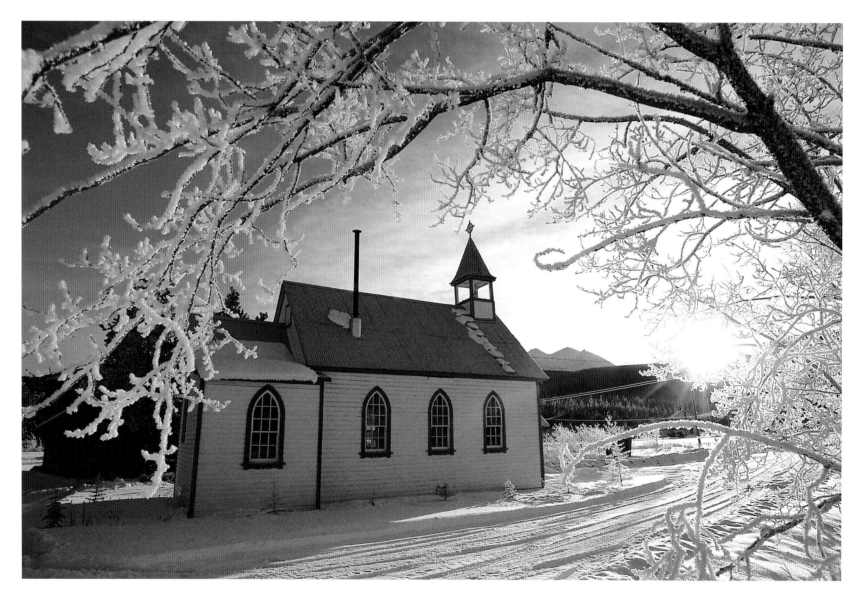

St. Saviours' Church in Carcross was constructed in 1902.

The S.S. Tutshi was lost to fire a few months after this photo was taken. Years earlier fire also destroyed two other sternwheelers in Whitehorse. This leaves the territory with only two of these historic relics; two from a fleet that once numbered in the hundreds.

Carcross, its name derived from Caribou Crossing, was a main stop for the White Pass and Yukon Route Railway. The narrow gauge train was built just after the gold rush and later hauled ore from Yukon mines to tidewater at Skagway, Alaska. The construction of the Carcross-Skagway Road made rail transportation uneconomical. The train made its last run into the territory in 1982.

The Carcross Desert, affection-ately known as the smallest desert in the world, was once the bottom of a glacial lake.

A log cabin boasts a well-tended flower box.

The wall of an old log structure forms a backdrop for a field of fireweed, Yukon's floral emblem.

As spring meltwater runs down the rocks along the Carcross-Skagway Road, picturesque layers of icicles are formed.

Winter winds mold snow into modern sculpture.

A rainbow forms over Windy Arm on Tagish Lake.

Winds drop and a sunbeam strikes the mountains on the far shore.

A ripple free Windy Arm.

Fireweed, backlit by a golden sunset.

A lone canoeist makes his way down Teslin Lake on a hot summer afternoon.

The Teslin River is pictured from Johnson's Crossing Bridge.The bridge was built high enough to permit sternwheeler traffic to pass unencumbered.

A plant forms its own abstract art.

Canol reflections.

Dew brightens
the leaves of a
wild rose bush.

Old construction equipment adds a touch of history to the Canol Road. Oil barrels, telephone lines and other things potentially harmful to wildlife have been removed, but a number of the vehicles remain.

A bull moose during the rut.

A cow moose enjoys a meal of water plants before freeze-up changes her diet to willow shoots.

Macabre beauty.

Hoar frost against a cobalt sky.

Ice pans begin to form in the Yukon River.

Freeze-up on Fox Lake.

The tents of the Story Telling Festival brighten Rotary Peace Park in Whitehorse.
Each June the festival draws "those with a tale to tell" from all around the world.

Main Street and the downtown area of Whitehorse, Yukon's capital city.

The moon rises over the restored S.S. Klondike.

As winter temperatures plummet, the aurora borealis sweeps over the Takhini River.

As the winter sun burns off the ice fog, Whitehorse's Second Avenue sparkles.

The Yukon River, still open, causes ice crystals to coat the Yukon Government Building and all its surroundings.

Dog teams take off down First Avenue in Whitehorse, the start of the 1,800 kilometre Yukon Quest race to Fairbanks, Alaska.

A future musher?

Evening, as the moon rises over the mountains, can be one of the most beautiful times in the Yukon.

A dog team crosses Lake Laberge. Mushing is a popular pastime in the territory. Small, fun teams are kept just for weekend outings, and large kennels train teams for thousand-mile races.

Tarfu Lake, near the British Columbia border.

Alpine Arnica, one of hundreds of hardy northern plants that add colour to the Yukon landscape.

The midnight sun gilds Teslin Lake. Although the sun does set during the summer in the southern Yukon, days are long enough that it is possible to sit outside and read a newspaper at 11 p.m. or go fishing at midnight.

Yukon sunsets are long and can be spectacular. This one is over Little Atlin Lake.

The narrow valleys and brilliant fall foliage have placed the Canol Road on the "must see" list of many photographers. The reds of buckbrush and Bear Berry along the Rose River are small samples of the palette available.

Numerous small ponds along the Canol add interesting, different perspectives for photographers, artists and those who enjoy the autumn scenery.

Nature's patterns.

Order out of chaos.

Crisp, frosty mornings show the Canol landscape at its best.

A young coyote prepares for an evening hunt.

Porcupine can be plentiful throughout much of the territory.

Repetitious pattern and unique northern
light produce unusual images.

Autumn fog makes its way down the Midnight Dome in
Dawson City. Cool fall mornings often form mist that
envelopes the historic center for the early part of the day.

A truck winds through the Richardson Range on the Dempster Highway. The road provides a surface link for communities north of the Arctic Circle.

Word of the splendid (but often short-lived) autumn colour along the Dempster Highway is out and the area now draws photographers from around the world. Peak colour is usually about the first of September.

Chapman Lake, along the Dempster.

Mountains along the Dempster vary from rugged spires to large softly rolling hills. This provides many photographic possibilities.

All the gold in the
Yukon is not buried
in the ground.

One of the few remaining cabins along the Hunker Creek Road. In spite of modern mining activity the Klondike still contains many historic artifacts.

World famous because of the Klondike Gold Rush of 1898, Dawson City is still a bustling placer mining, can-can kicking community. The George Black Ferry is pictured in the background as it crosses the Yukon River, connecting traffic to the Top-of-the-World Highway.

The Klondike River Valley is a mass of gravel tailings left by gigantic dredges that stripped river bottoms down to bedrock in search of gold.

The old repair shop at Bear Creek, where mining equipment was kept operational. It is now preserved as a National Historic Site.

Several old dredges remain in various stages of disrepair throughout the Klondike. Some have been cannibalized for parts for present-day gold mining, one or two have been restored to working use, and another has been preserved by Parks Canada as an historic site.

The S.S. Keno rests on the banks of the Yukon River in Dawson City. Pictured in the foreground is the Bank of Commerce, where the bard, Robert Service, worked to pay the bills while writing his famous poetry about life in the north.

The Palace Grand Theatre has been reconstructed to the luxuriance of the original structure built by Arizona Charlie Meadows in 1898. Many of the town's old buildings have been refurbished to maintain gold rush character.

Juno-winning Jerry Alfred performs for a home audience.

Entertainers from all over Canada travel to the Klondike
to take part in the annual Dawson City Music Festival.

Tom Byrne reads each summer as the "Spirit of Robert Service" in front of the Service cabin. Over the years he has spent more time at the cabin than the bard himself.

Inside the restored Robert Service cabin.

A sundog, formed by sunlight reflecting off ice crystals in the air, adds soft colour to a cold winter day.

OVERLEAF – **H**ardy Yukoners find homes all over the territory. Some, such as these on the Fish Lake Road near Whitehorse, favour spots where they can enjoy rural beauty without the rigors of true wilderness living.